JUNIOR BIOGRAPHIES

Kathy Furgang

OPRAH WINFREY

BUSINESSWOMAN AND ACTRESS

Enslow Publishing
101 W. 23rd Street
Suite 240
New York, NY 10011
USA

enslow.com

WORDS TO KNOW

ambitious Working hard to get ahead and succeed.

assault An attack.

cohost A person who leads or entertains, sharing the duty with someone else.

councilman A person who is elected to help make decisions for a town or city.

deprived Poor, needy.

entrepreneur A person who starts, organizes, or operates businesses.

influential Having a strong power or effect.

nominated Recommended for an award.

scholarship Money that is awarded to help someone pay for school.

CONTENTS

Oprah Winfrey

CHAPTER 1

OPRAH AS A CHILD

She's one of the most famous celebrities in the world. She's often known by just her first name—Oprah. She rose to fame as a talk show host and is today one of the most influential media personalities in the world. But Oprah Winfrey had to overcome a difficult childhood. She started out a long way from the life of wealth she knows today.

A DIFFICULT BEGINNING

Oprah Gail Winfrey was born on January 29, 1954, on a farm in Kosciusko, Mississippi. Oprah's mother, Vernita Lee, was only 18 when she gave birth to Oprah. Her father, Vernon Winfrey, was 20. Vernita worked as a maid. Vernon was a coal miner and a barber. He eventually became a city councilman.

FIRST HOME SITE OF
• Oprah Winfrey •

KOSCIUSKO, MISSISSIPPI

On January 29, 1954, Oprah Winfrey was born in a wood frame house located on this site to Mr. and Mrs. Vernon Winfrey. She resided here as a child before moving to Milwaukee at age six. Within walking distance is the church where she made her first appearance in an Easter recitation.

She grew in the information/entertainment industry to become the world's foremost TV talk show host with a daily audience in the millions. At the same time she never forgot or overlooked her heritage and has been a regular supporter of folks back home as well as a role model to much of America.

A sign stands in the area where Oprah was born in Kosciusko, Mississippi. The road there has been renamed Oprah Winfrey Road.

Oprah Says:

"I learned to read at age three and soon discovered there was a whole world to conquer that went beyond our farm in Mississippi."

A YOUNG READER

Growing up, Oprah had a very difficult life. Her parents separated after she was born. Her grandmother, Hattie Mae Lee, often took care of her. Her grandmother was very strict. She frequently beat Oprah. However, she taught Oprah to read and write at age three.

When Oprah entered kindergarten, she wrote a note to her teacher. She wrote that she belonged in the first grade. It worked. The teacher allowed her to skip to first grade.

When Oprah was young, she moved around a lot. At six, she moved with her mother and other family members to a poor and dangerous neighborhood in Milwaukee, Wisconsin. The next year, she moved to Nashville, Tennessee, to live with her father. The following year, Oprah moved yet again. She returned to Milwaukee to live with her mother again. Through all of the moves, Oprah read books. They helped her see all of the possibilities in the world.

Chapter 2
A Serious Student

Things got very bad for Oprah while she lived with her mother in Milwaukee. She was sexually assaulted by several people trusted by the family. The abuse went on for years. She was afraid to tell anyone about it. By the time Oprah was 13, she did not know where to turn for help. She even became pregnant and tried to hide it.

Oprah ran away from home to escape her problems. At 14, she gave birth to a son. He died after just a few weeks.

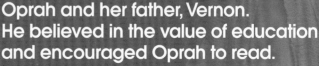

Oprah and her father, Vernon. He believed in the value of education and encouraged Oprah to read.

It was around this time that Oprah told her father that she had been abused. She then went to live with him and his wife.

Oprah Says:

"My father's insistence that education was the open door to freedom is what allows me to stand here today a free woman."

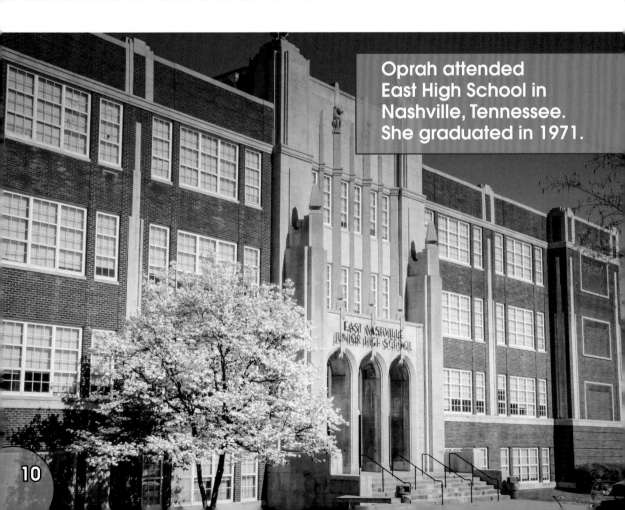

Oprah attended East High School in Nashville, Tennessee. She graduated in 1971.

THE ROAD AHEAD

Oprah's life began to improve when she went to live with her father and stepmother. She finally had the structure and support she needed. She read a lot and made weekly book reports. The book reports were in addition to her regular schoolwork. Her father also made her learn at least five new vocabulary words each day before dinner.

> At college, Winfrey majored in speech communications and performing arts.

Oprah was very ambitious at school. She loved public speaking. She joined the drama club and the debate club at her high school. In her senior year, she won a speaking contest. Because of that, she won a full scholarship to Tennessee State University. The next year, a Nashville radio station hired her to read the news.

CHAPTER 3
TALK SHOW STAR POWER

After Oprah graduated college, she took a job at a TV station in Baltimore, Maryland. She worked as a co-anchor on the news. She did a good job. Soon she was hired as a **cohost** on a talk show called *People Are Talking*.

Oprah's next job was in Chicago, Illinois. She became a cohost on a show called *AM Chicago*. It became so successful that it was renamed *The Oprah Winfrey Show* in September 1985. The show went national. This meant people all around the country saw it. On *The Oprah Winfrey Show*, Oprah interviewed guests and spoke about important topics. It quickly became the number one talk show in the country.

In 1978, Oprah was hired as a cohost for a local Baltimore talk show called *People Are Talking*. She was an immediate success.

AN INSPIRATION

Oprah's success caught the attention of people all around the world. Famous people chose to be interviewed by her. She interviewed important people in the news. People felt comfortable talking to her.

The show won 16 Daytime Emmy Awards for Outstanding Talk Show and Outstanding Talk Show Host between the years 1987 and 1998. She also became the youngest person to win the International Radio and Television Society's Broadcaster of the Year Award.

Oprah Says:

"I don't think of myself as a poor deprived ghetto girl who made good. I think of myself as somebody who from an early age knew I was responsible for myself, and I had to make good."

Oprah interviews a young Will Smith, star of *The Fresh Prince of Bel-Air*, in 1992.

Oprah looks on as President Bill Clinton signs the National Child Protection Act in 1993. The act created a database to track child abusers.

Soon after *The Oprah Winfrey Show* started, Oprah started her own production company, Harpo Inc. "Harpo" is "Oprah" spelled backward.

MORE THAN JUST TALK

Oprah was now a true celebrity. She was able to choose important projects that meant a lot to her. One of those projects was the 1985 film *The Color Purple.* The film was about a girl growing up in the South in the early 1900s. It was Oprah's first time acting in a movie. She was nominated in the Best Supporting Actress category for both an Oscar and a Golden Globe Award.

In 1993, Oprah spoke in front of a group of United States senators. She asked for a national database to search for child abusers. President Bill Clinton signed the "Oprah Bill" into law on December 20 of that year. The law was called the National Child Protection Act.

CHAPTER 4
A BUSINESS EMPIRE

Oprah became more and more successful. People listened to what she had to say. If she recommended a book or a product, people bought it. Oprah became an **entrepreneur** by starting new businesses. In 2000, she started a monthly magazine called *O, The Oprah Magazine.* The magazine was a way to appeal to and reach people who watched her talk show. In 2003, Oprah became the first African American female billionaire.

In 2000, Oprah posed with the first issue of *O* at a party celebrating the new magazine.

Oprah speaks about OWN at a 2011 event. Through the network's programs, she hopes to encourage people to "live their best life."

In 2011, Oprah ended her talk show after 25 years. She wanted to do more in business and entertainment. That same year, she started OWN, the Oprah Winfrey Network. The cable television channel has original shows and interviews with celebrities.

Oprah Says:

"Unless you choose to do great things with it, it makes no difference how much you are rewarded, or how much power you have."

Oprah celebrates the first graduating class at the Leadership Academy for Girls in South Africa.

The students at the Leadership Academy for Girls refer to Oprah as "Mama-O."

Building a Future

One of Oprah's biggest concerns for the future is education. In 2000, she donated $10 million to schools in South Africa. Oprah continued to work to improve the education of girls in South Africa. In 2007, she opened the Leadership Academy for Girls in a small town near Johannesburg, South Africa. Oprah uses her own money to keep much of the school running. She enjoys being part of the projects that help the students become strong leaders.

Oprah came from humble and difficult beginnings. Her rise to fame inspired many. And throughout her life, she has remembered to give back to the community.

TIMELINE

1954 Oprah Winfrey is born on January 29 in Kosciusko, Mississippi.

1959 Writes a note to her kindergarten teacher and asks to skip a grade.

1976 Takes a job at a Baltimore radio station after college.

1984 Becomes a cohost of *AM Chicago* in Chicago, Illinois.

1985 *AM Chicago* is renamed *The Oprah Winfrey Show* and reaches a national audience.

2000 Starts *O* Magazine.

2003 Becomes the first African American female billionaire.

2007 Opens the Leadership Academy for Girls in South Africa.

2011 Starts OWN, the Oprah Winfrey Network.

2013 Is awarded the Presidential Medal of Freedom by Barack Obama.

2018 Becomes the first African American woman to win the Golden Globe Cecil B. DeMille Award for her contributions to the entertainment world.

BOOKS

Baby Professor. *From Rags to Riches: The Oprah Winfrey Story*. Newark, DE: Speedy Publishing, 2017.

Mara, Wil. *Oprah Winfrey: An Inspiration to Millions*. New York, NY: Scholastic Publishing, 2016.

Moss, Caroline. *Oprah Winfrey: Run the Show Like CEO*. London, UK: Lincoln Children's Books, 2019.

WEBSITES

Ducksters: Oprah Winfrey

www.ducksters.com/biography/entertainers/oprah_winfrey.php

Learn facts about Oprah and take a quiz about her life!

Kiddle: Oprah Winfrey Facts

kids.kiddle.co/Oprah_Winfrey

Read about Oprah on Kiddle, an online encyclopedia for kids.

Oprah's Reading List for Kids

www.oprah.com/oprahsbookclub/kids-reading-list

See what Oprah recommends for child readers at different age levels.

INDEX

Published in 2020 by Enslow Publishing, LLC.
101 W. 23rd Street, Suite 240, New York, NY 10011

Library of Congress Cataloging-in-Publication Data
Names: Furgang, Kathy, author.
Title: Oprah Winfrey : businesswoman and actress / Kathy Furgang.
Description: New York : Enslow Publishing, 2020. | Series: Junior biographies
Audience: Grades 3-5. | Includes bibliographical references and index.
Identifiers: LCCN 2018052889| ISBN 9781978507470 (library bound) | ISBN 9781978508989 (pbk.) | ISBN 9781978508996 (6 pack)
Subjects: LCSH: Winfrey, Oprah—Juvenile literature. | Television personalities—United States—Biography—Juvenile literature. | Actors—United States—Biography—Juvenile literature. | Businesswomen—United States—Biography.
Classification: LCC PN1992.4.W56 F87 2019 | DDC 791.4502/8092 [B] —dc23
LC record available at https://lccn.loc.gov/2018052889

Printed in the United States of America

To Our Readers: We have done our best to make sure all website addresses in this book were active and appropriate when we went to press. However, the author and the publisher have no control over and assume no liability for the material available on those websites or on any websites they may link to. Any comments or suggestions can be sent by e-mail to customerservice@enslow.com.

Photos Credits: Cover, p. 1 Jim Spellman/WireImage/Getty Images; p. 4 Jeff Vespa/WireImage/Getty Images; p. 6 Stuart Abraham/Alamy Stock Photo; p. 9 Adriane Jaeckle/Getty Images; p. 10 Jennifer Wright/Alamy Stock Photo; p. 13 Afro Newspaper/Gado/Archive Photos/Getty Images; p. 15 © NBC/Courtesy: Everett Collection; p. 16 © AP Images; p. 18 Evan Agostini/Hulton Archive/Getty Images; p. 19 Frederick M. Brown/Getty Images; p. 20 Michelly Rall/Getty Images; interior page bottoms (red carpet graphic) Sashkin/Shutterstock.com.